RISK MANAGEMENT STRATEGIES IN SCHOOL DEVELOPMENT

DR DHEERAJ MEHROTRA

Contents

Preface

Establishing risk management solutions improves the overall management quality of safe schools. Culture, administration, and psychological counselling are crucial to the success of safe schools. Attempts at enhancing the quality begin with a thorough analysis of current conditions, including a close watch for potential dangers and a detailed look at strengths and shortcomings.

Implementing rules and methods for a school's culture cannot be limited to the classroom. Establishing risk management and other laws and procedures may improve school culture and quality. The book "RISK MANAGEMENT STRATEGIES IN SCHOOL DEVELOPMENT" is one of the initiatives toward mastering the challenge.

Cheers & Happy learning.

www.authordheerajmehrotra.com

CHAPTER ONE

Understanding Risk Management in Schools

MVP
52

When it comes to the administration of a school, the fundamental vocabulary of quality focuses on risk management, which encompasses prospective pitfalls while avoiding actual dangers. Consequently, the formulation of plans and policies is of utmost significance for the management of risks.

A significant amount of work is required to achieve quality, and the first stage in this process is the observation of risks and the identification of both weaknesses and strengths. The purpose of this study is to analyse risk management as well as appropriate techniques and policies for dealing with hazards in the educational environment. The school's culture reflects the school as a whole, and risk management is a process that helps schools improve their overall performance. In this study, we focused on obtaining a qualitative quality. Interviews were conducted with both directors and assistant directors to clarify the policies and strategies associated with risk management.

The following investigation must ensure quality at its place, viz., school culture, school strategies, school policies, and risk management. Students are put in danger by several circumstances as a result of the rapid advancement of technology and the rising enrollment numbers in schools. Concerns on a psychological level, a hostile and fictitious environment, the presence of technology, and a propensity toward violent behaviour are these variables. The idea of violence is something that people are exposed to at every stage of their lives, and as a result, everyone has come to accept it.

Safety schools can increase the degree of management they give by using various risk management strategies. The functioning of safe schools is significantly impacted by multiple factors, including culture, management, and psychological orientation. Because of this, it has become more important

for educational institutions to emphasise strategic planning to bring the quality of their administrative practices into line with quality requirements.

The school's administration needs to significantly focus on risk management as the essential quality term to provide the best possible education for the students. Identifying and avoiding potential issues is integral to risk management, which occurs before taking on real threats. Consequently, developing strategies and executing policies are both necessary components of risk management. The first step in establishing quality entails focusing primarily on maintaining vigilance concerning prospective threats and researching existing strengths and opportunities for improvement.

Within the scope of this research is an analysis of risk management in schools and an examination of current strategies and policies for addressing the dangers inherent in educational institutions' ethos. This form of study is known as qualitative research. Interviews were held with principals and vice principals of various schools to gather information on their experiences. The approach of thematic analysis was used to research the following subjects: the culture of schools, the strategy and policy of schools, and risk management. The outcomes of the study indicate that both Principals and Vice-Principals have expertise in risk management.

It is not sufficient to implement regulations and procedures to establish a culture inside a school successfully. It has been shown that by setting risk management practices and creating extra rules and procedures, an educational institution's culture and overall quality may be enhanced. In schools, violence can manifest itself in a variety of ways, including but not limited to the following: cursing at other people; inflicting physical harm on other people; making threats against other people; acting tough toward other people and attempting to exert dominance over them by pushing, hitting, and fighting; threatening someone with toy guns; abusing; inflicting harm with a knife; or consuming alcohol while

forcing other people to attend classes.

CHAPTER TWO

SAFETY & SECURITY ANCHORS

Every school must have some Risk Management Strategies to promote safety and security. Plans should be established based on school locations, natural resources, and dangers. Because the origin and extent of natural and human-oriented risks and threats cannot be predicted in advance, protective and preventative actions must be taken to reduce damages. If a school is involved, it should respond quickly and correctly.

The following are some of the Safety and Security Anchors which are a priority and should be in place.

SAFETY & SECURITY ANCHOR

OBJ

#1

School buildings must be monitored around the clock every single day. Check that all your

CCTV cameras are operational and set to record at the appropriate rate. A dimensional picture of the recorded data has to be analysed regularly to guarantee accuracy by the admin officers, vice principals, principals and management. The results need to be explored, and questions need to be asked about them with the students' overall interest in mind.

SAFETY & SECURITY ANCHOR

#2

It is required that there be emergency evacuation preparations in place.
Every level is required to have a visible ENTRY plan and an EXIT plan. To calm the pupils, check the locks and barricades and ensure that qualified armed guards are on duty. Make sure a sign that identifies an official gathering place inside the school is visible to the public. A meeting point is a predetermined area considered safe and serves as a location where students may congregate or are required to report in an emergency, for example, or during a fire drill.

SAFETY & SECURITY ANCHOR
#3

Appoint senior students to serve as FLOOR leaders so that a smooth traffic flow may be managed class-wise during recesses, before and after assemblies, and while students leave the school. Each building level must have a TEACHER on duty and be equipped with a tiny staff room staffed by instructors responsible for teaching lessons on that particular floor. An educator with free time throughout the school day is obligated to keep a close check on the children in their classroom if they leave for any reason.

SAFETY & SECURITY ANCHOR

#4

Schools may protect student safety by preparing pupils to maintain their composure in the event of an assault. This is something that has to be worked on regularly with MOCK Drills. Ensure that everyone has access to a high-quality education that is inclusive and egalitarian, and encourage people to continue their education throughout their lives. The youngsters must be given simulated sessions to cope with circumstances like this. They should refrain from reacting and contribute to a safe evacuation without fear or worry.

SAFETY & SECURITY ANCHOR

#5

There needs to be consistent monitoring of hazing and bullying. Class Monitors need to be trained to report any inappropriate behaviour to the Head of the School in a confidential setting. Teachers need to be indisputable partners, the front-line players to whom students may confidently turn for assistance, encouragement, and inspiration as they stand on the brink of entering their teenage years. The children need to feel as if their professors are members of their own extended families.

SAFETY & SECURITY ANCHOR

#6

Teachers' relationships with the children and the student's parents must be managed appropriately. Monitoring will be recorded using the INTERACTION Register to make safety a PRIORITY in the process. Parents must submit a family portrait with their kids at the centre for safety and security purposes. This helps ensure proper communication and networking. This record leads to a better understanding of the child's family and themselves.

SAFETY & SECURITY ANCHOR

#7

Counsellors and psychologists should be employed in schools to assist pupils in overcoming difficulties related to traumatic experiences, anger, and sadness. The goal should be to instil in them not just a set of ideals but also a feeling of moral duty and a sense of belonging to their country. The teacher is the one who knows the kid the best and can shape the youngster according to the most effective framework and criteria. Every student is required to get from their TEACHER objective guidance that is devoid of AWE.

SAFETY & SECURITY ANCHOR

#8

Students need to be able to take care of themselves and respond appropriately to circumstances such as being abused or kidnapped, and schools need to teach them these skills. Ensure that money is spent on teaching individuals and providing them with tools to combat child abuse and POCSO, also known as The Protection of Children from Sexual Offences Act (POCSO Act). The school administration must hold at least two seminars on CHILD ABUSE during each session.

SAFETY & SECURITY ANCHOR

#9

Schools must guarantee that the food served

to students on school grounds (whether in the school cafeteria or a school mess) adheres to the appropriate hygienic standards and rules. To guarantee that the food given in schools is safe for human consumption, the food's quality must be routinely evaluated.

SAFETY & SECURITY ANCHOR #10

The technology included in smartphones may be used to benefit an educational institution to ensure the student's safety and well-being. Investigate the possibility of researching and adopting the use of BLOCKCHAIN technology to improve the safety of students on campus. There is also the possibility of using artificial intelligence and augmented reality. The use of technology is thus necessary for the smooth operation of a school.

SAFETY & SECURITY ANCHOR

#11

Put EFFECTIVE CCTV Cameras in every nook and cranny of the school grounds, including the entrances to the WASH ROOMS and the points of access and departure into the school. It is recommended that it be put in every classroom and that the parents be provided access to the stream through an application for mobile devices.

SAFETY & SECURITY ANCHOR

#12

The School Compound Ought to Have a Gated Fencing Surrounding It. Guards need to be on ROUND duty, equipped with the appropriate lattice and torch and should blow a whistle. Additionally, the GPRS tracking system needs to be used to keep an eye on the different positions of this security personnel.

SAFETY & SECURITY ANCHOR

#13

At the School Gate, There Ought to Be Security Personnel Who Can MONITOR the CCTV Camera, and They Ought to Do This Round-the-Clock. The ENTRY and the EXIT entries on the Entry/Exit REGISTER need to be marked and adequately signed regularly.

SAFETY & SECURITY ANCHOR

#14

Before entering the school premises, the person responsible for the MEETING is the only one who should provide clearance to any visitor. During regularly scheduled Parent-Teacher Conferences, teachers must keep vigil in front of classroom doors to monitor students for any signs of inappropriate behaviour.

SAFETY & SECURITY ANCHOR

#15

Students and employees should always have their identification cards and any valid security IDs on their person. Law enforcement agents must be granted the right to carry out random and preventative searches of students' personal belongings and lockers. In addition to this, a check on driving licences and automobiles is required to be maintained.

SAFETY & SECURITY ANCHOR

#16

Before hiring any staff, including teachers and other employees, a comprehensive background check has to be performed. During an employee's employment, schools must perform routine background checks on that individual's criminal history. In addition, the institution is obligated to develop regulations that require school personnel to notify any arrests for crimes to their respective school employees within twenty-four hours of the arrests in question.

SAFETY & SECURITY ANCHOR

#17

Students need to get training on a variety of security-related topics, incidents, and scenarios. It is essential for kids' personal and social growth that schools provide an environment conducive to both. Everyone on the faculty and in the student body should know what to do in a CRISIS. There must be coordination with the POLICE.

SAFETY & SECURITY ANCHOR

#18

In the school, there should be a Leadership Team and a Security Club, both of which should have REGULAR safety and security requirements. Every conceivable kind of person from the school, the neighbourhood, and outside need to be represented on the squad. These persons are responsible for analysing the needs assessment, coming up with both short-term and long-term objectives, and developing school-wide preventative measures.

SAFETY & SECURITY ANCHOR

OBJ

#19

Students shouldn't be allowed to be picked up from school by anybody other than their parents or someone who has been appropriately assigned to do so. The staff has to be taught to recognise the parents, and this training ensures that the school's comprehensive violence prevention strategy is understood, supported, and used. Because of the ongoing training, the students and the instructors are more at ease with the emergency procedure.

SAFETY & SECURITY ANCHOR

OBJ

#20

The school premises must be outfitted with a central security alarm system. It is necessary to do a simulated exercise for the same purpose regularly. Mass notification, emergency communication, an indicator of any terrorist attack, and everything in between need to be included in any comprehensive and integrated security solution. This includes intrusion detection security systems, video surveillance, and fire alarm test and inspections.

SAFETY & SECURITY ANCHOR

OBJ

#21

To prevent students from bringing potentially lethal weapons into school grounds, it is necessary to conduct random bag checks on the students. These random searches have to be based on particular needs that apply to the whole school, such as making sure the school is secure, and they have to be completely random. It is not permissible to conduct a search at random to find any particular student at the school.

SAFETY & SECURITY ANCHOR

#22

It is necessary to keep a close eye on the activities of students in order to prevent their participation in covert organisations. It is necessary to keep a close eye on the children's unique characteristics while providing them with consistent incentives and positive reinforcement. Only if the kid has a strong connection to the Teacher will this be feasible. Activating the potential for growth in the classroom is accomplished via monitoring.

SAFETY & SECURITY ANCHOR

OBJ

#23

Students should be encouraged to report any suspicious activity or person they see on school grounds to the school's administration. The progression of a kid's development is something that instructors should collaborate on with other educators with whom the child will be interacting in the grade that follows theirs. It is of the utmost importance that we prioritise the provision of a variety of different reporting alternatives, such as anonymous reporting tactics via websites, text, and phones, as well as through specially designated instructors and counsellors and peers.

SAFETY & SECURITY ANCHOR

OBJ

#24

Students should only be permitted to leave the

school grounds if they have a pass from the security post. This rule should be strictly enforced. Without the previous permission of a parent or guardian, it is unacceptable for a youngster to be permitted to go home alone. Once the children have left the school's grounds, the obligation to monitor them shifts from the school to the parents, and the parents need to be aware of this shift in responsibility.

SAFETY & SECURITY ANCHOR

#25

People should be discouraged from loitering outside the school gate or parking their cars. The schools should make it easier for parents to drop off and pick up their children by encouraging them to use the carpooling system. This may bring to less confusion in the traffic outside of schools and also make it easier for cars to circulate. It is of the utmost importance to blend in with the society, public, and neighbourhood at the junction to facilitate effortless commerce and transport, all while maintaining a secure environment.

SAFETY & SECURITY ANCHOR

#26

The issue centres on whether or not students should be allowed to use mobile phones in school-related settings or situations. Inside the School Building, Students should not be permitted to use their Mobile Phones in any Capacity. There should not be any kind of blanket ban on phones, but children should be able to use them in an emergency. They should only be allowed access to a cell phone if they are required to make urgent contact with their parents or legal guardians.

SAFETY & SECURITY ANCHOR

#27

Access cards that use biometric technology and can be recognised by students and their parents need to be issued. This system can be used for the purchase of food and drink in the dining hall, as well as for the use in the library to manage the loan of books and the submission of books that were issued earlier using recognition, and for the service in use in the dining hall to manage the purchase of food and drink in the dining hall.

SAFETY & SECURITY ANCHOR

#28

Children should be instructed not to initiate a conversation with anybody they do not know, whether they are on or outside the school grounds. Because of the sad instances of our students being kidnapped and molested inside and outside the schools, it is even more vital that we educate our children about Mr Dangerous Stranger and teach them how and why they should be watchful throughout their whole lives.

SAFETY & SECURITY ANCHOR

#29

Train educators to look for problems such as cyberbullying, child abuse, and racism in their classrooms. A session on identifying and reporting child abuse is an absolute need. Parents and teachers must put the Child Abuse

Identification and Reporting Workshop at the top of their to-do lists.

SAFETY & SECURITY ANCHOR

#30

As part of the ROUTINE activity, instruct students about the emergency protocols that the school follows via simulation games, mock drills, and YouTube videos. Children need to be prepared to handle any kind of emergency. SUPW periods must include online drilling sessions as a form of regular training and preparation.

SAFETY & SECURITY ANCHOR

#31

Instruct students on the travel routes to and from the school for nearby sites. Children and staff should be on the lookout for assistance, and the school's POICE and relief/help/ emergency number must be marked appropriately and restricted in every nook and corner of the campus.

SAFETY & SECURITY ANCHOR

#32

All parties involved must have a solid understanding of the preventative and detective measures used at the institution. In the event of an unexpected catastrophe, all parties involved must consistently get an orientation about any new building and a handbook and video detailing the facility's departure and entrance procedures.

SAFETY & SECURITY ANCHOR

#33

When considering learning as a whole, the

environment is the most important factor. It is attainable by emphasising three distinct aspects: the instructors, the instructional materials, and the available technology. In the Finland Model, the training of teachers is an essential component, alongside the development of innovative and individualised curricula. The Indian education system is built on rote memorization, which only develops parrots, not creative thinkers. Exams are also based on rote memorization.

SAFETY & SECURITY ANCHOR

#34

The staff needs to be updated on student safety concerns and behavioural issues regularly. Instead of limiting their connection with a class to a single school year, instructors should monitor the growth of the students as they go through the grades. The whole teaching and learning process needs to take place inside a setting described as "facilitating," which is not an accessible environment to produce. Just have a look at the atmosphere in the house. It is all about exercising control and obeying orders. This is where the education of our children begins. Therefore, the family environment, the educational environment, and the society's ideals must be in sync to establish the Finland system.

SAFETY & SECURITY ANCHOR

#35

Urgent attention must be paid to any loose electrical wires. Suppose there is a short circuit or loose wiring anywhere on campus. In that case, the administrator, staff member, prefect, or student council representative on floor duty must notify the appropriate authorities.

SAFETY & SECURITY ANCHOR

#36

Audits of the school building's structural integrity should be performed regularly. To be prepared for any emergency, the fire alarms and fighting equipment must be examined to ensure they are in place and functioning. This is something that has to be checked with MOCK Drills, both on and off.

SAFETY & SECURITY ANCHOR

#37

The Schools are responsible for ensuring that the railings and paths along the staircases and corridors are in good structural condition. During the dispersion process, they need to be brightly illuminated and supervised by an adult. To guarantee a smooth and risk-free traffic flow to and from the school boundary, separate entry points for pedestrians and motorists should be established whenever and wherever feasible.

Before entering a school's grounds, a visitor may get a good idea of how seriously the institution takes matters of safety and security just by seeing the fence encircles the campus and the gates leading to the main entrance.

SAFETY & SECURITY ANCHOR

#38

The school's bathroom facilities protect students' privacy and keep them secure. Going to a school deficient in basic amenities like bathrooms may be one of the most aggravating experiences for many people; as a result, entry to the restrooms has to be supervised. Using CCTV cameras, every movement a student makes while in one of the unattended or restricted areas must be monitored and examined.

SAFETY & SECURITY ANCHOR

#39

Students in elementary school, high school, and college all need to be able to provide a valid school ID card to demonstrate that they are enrolled in the appropriate educational institution.
Assure that the SOCIAL and EMOTIONAL needs of the children are met via PEP discussions and interactions, which may involve home visits by the teachers. Badges and name tags must be essential for the NON-TEACHING STAFF and the TEACHING STAFF.

SAFETY & SECURITY ANCHOR

#40

It is essential that both the teaching and non-teaching staff members undergo police verification at all times. As a kind of recorded information, this may also involve a check of the cultural background of the stakeholders as well as their parents' backgrounds. Another rule is to ensure that support workers are only hired from authorised agencies and that adequate records are kept. This is one of the requirements.

SAFETY & SECURITY ANCHOR

#41

CBSE Quote
"Schools are required to have psychometric testing done on all of the faculty and employees. This kind of verification and assessment for non-teaching employees, such as bus drivers, conductors, peons, and other support staff, may be carried out in an extremely rigorous and specific way." A psychometric evaluation of the teaching and non-teaching staff must be carried out at all times.

SAFETY & SECURITY ANCHOR

#42

The playground must have an appealing visual design and should be maintained regularly. It should also provide chances for many courts and sports that include physical activity at different skill levels. Ensure that the attendance of every kid is noted three times a day and that notifications are given a home to parents if any of their children are missing. Ensure that no kid is ever disciplined in a manner that might result in either mental or bodily harm to the child.

SAFETY & SECURITY ANCHOR

#43

It is required that the classrooms have an aesthetically pleasing design and fully equipped information and communication technology facilities and support mechanisms. Licenses for the software being used should have regular updates performed on it, as should anti-virus software, and computers should have firewalls placed so that cyberbullying may be prevented.

SAFETY & SECURITY ANCHOR

#44

A verification that there are sufficient TOILETS explicitly designated for boys and girls as well as male and female staff members, clean drinking water, a medical room, and a counselling room. Separate washrooms for boys and girls, located at an appropriate distance from one another, and the presence of a female attendant in the girls' washroom are two of the preventative measures that have been proposed to ensure the protection of females.

SAFETY & SECURITY ANCHOR

#45

Every single student has to have access to psychiatric support as well as counselling, especially with the issue of cyberbullying. School counsellors must provide study skills workshops, lessons on sexual education, and information sessions for pupils about bullying. They HAVE TO work with the instructors, the parents, and the special educators to construct an educational setting that is conducive to their well-being and allows them to feel at ease.

SAFETY & SECURITY ANCHOR

#46

Buses should adhere to explicit rules for various factors, such as the ratio of seats to students, the display of emergency numbers, and the monitoring system. If a girl has to leave school for an exam or another function, she should have a female teacher or attendant accompany her. Additionally, the female attendant on the school bus should not get off the vehicle until all of the girls have been delivered to their final destination.

SAFETY & SECURITY ANCHOR

#47

Following the various stages, aesthetic, well-designed furniture that is also developmentally suitable should be placed in classrooms. The design of the school building needs to have enough natural light and air movement throughout.

SAFETY & SECURITY ANCHOR

#48

It is recommended that a school safety committee be formed to ensure and monitor the implementation of safety practices within the school. The extra duty for the student's safety and security needs to be delegated to the Student Council, and they ought to be instructed to take on this role. Additionally, the school has to establish a watchdog committee made up of parents, and the schools need to make sure they follow what the committee recommends.

SAFETY & SECURITY ANCHOR

#49

The children from the schools pay a visit to the local police station to understand better the role that police play in our everyday lives and the contribution they make to the safety and security of the nation's residents.

According to the rules established by the boards and the government, schools must take safety concerns seriously.

SAFETY & SECURITY ANCHOR

#50

Visitor screenings using metal detectors need to take place consistently. Ensure that the people with a stake in the school are regularly prepared to handle crises and catastrophes. Give them plenty of practice by having them participate in mock drills and evacuation exercises.

SAFETY & SECURITY ANCHOR

#51

Every single laboratory in the school is required to have a written Safety Norm that has been established. Check to see if any facilities can accommodate pupils with varying degrees of ability. Students should no longer carry out laboratory work while their lecturers are absent. When they enter the science lab, students must have safety goggles, a lab coat, and shoes on at all times. In the scientific laboratories of schools, students should not be allowed to wear loose clothing or sandals or have their hair out in any way.

SAFETY & SECURITY ANCHOR

#52

Every student in the school, as well as every teacher and staff member, must be familiar with how to operate the fire fighting equipment on campus. Determine the TWO nearest exits as well as any feasible escape routes. Be familiar with the locations of the fire alarms and how to operate them. Vandalized fire safety equipment should be reported to campus security by both teachers and students.

SAFETY & SECURITY ANCHOR

#53

Cards must be filled out with the results of routine inspections of fire fighting equipment. Ensure that strict emergency management arrangements are in place for all fires and alarms during times of emergency, as well as a call for the closest police stations and mention any crucial phone numbers that need to be remembered.

SAFETY & SECURITY ANCHOR

#54

The student's intellectual, social, physical, and emotional requirements should all be addressed in the school's annual curriculum plan. Determine the potential dangers that might influence the area that your school and the surrounding region are located in. Determine the extent of the damage that each of the indicated hazards will cause.

Students and staff members need to be instructed on how to utilise the plan and what their roles will be in the event of a particular emergency.

SAFETY & SECURITY ANCHOR

#55

Always and everywhere, the infrastructure, which must include computer labs, science labs, and math labs, must be suitable for use and up to the anticipated standards. The areas where students gather while waiting for buses and the pedestrian walkways that connect those areas are large enough to accommodate everyone without becoming overcrowded. Every structure has a predetermined set of access points that may be used to govern who goes where. Determine a single point of entrance for guests, if at all practicable.

SAFETY & SECURITY ANCHOR

#56

To respond appropriately to medical and other emergent situations, the school must have suitable medical facilities and staff them with a nurse or doctor. Develop at least one Administrator Emergency Tool Kit for every one of your school's locations. Construct and disseminate emergency response manuals for each classroom. Establish and document procedures for providing students and staff access to mental health services.

SAFETY & SECURITY ANCHOR

#57

The restrooms, toilets, laboratories, playground, and classrooms need to be kept CLEAN, AIRY, and in good repair. In addition, schools must be equipped with ramps, they must accept students from underserved populations, and they should also have SPECIAL EDUCATORS available to assist those who are in need.

Sending at least two children into the restroom simultaneously ensures that if there is an unexpected complication, one of the children will be able to sound the alarm.

SAFETY & SECURITY ANCHOR

#58

There have to be separate TOILET ROOMS for the female staff members and the male staff members. The institution must also guarantee sufficient medical facilities and be prepared to deal with various medical and other emergent situations. In the absence of adequate cleaning, restrooms have the potential to become a fertile environment for the propagation of disease-causing bacteria across the student body.

SAFETY & SECURITY ANCHOR

#59

The Library needs to have enough ventilation and be provided with an EMERGENCY Alarm System and firefighting apparatus. Use posters and bulletin boards to draw attention to the possible risks and the precautions that should be taken. Put up readable and correct emergency contact information and procedures.

SAFETY & SECURITY ANCHOR

#60

The institution is obligated to demonstrate leadership in environmental preservation and significant leadership in implementing best practices for waste management. Composting may be taught to students via the use of organic waste. Compost may be used in school gardens, saving money for the schools that would otherwise be spent on fertiliser and other chemicals. Worm farms may be put up in schools, and then those farms might be utilised to teach various aspects of the curriculum.

SAFETY & SECURITY ANCHOR

#61

The institution of higher learning needs to provide a provision for individuals with varying degrees of ability should provide a supportive working environment with potential for advancement. Increasing numbers of students who use wheelchairs are enrolling in regular classes at public schools. The criteria for giving help to these children in schools must always be adhered to.

SAFETY & SECURITY ANCHOR

#62

It is necessary for there to be a feeling of SAFETY and SECURITY in the School, and there should be frequent evacuation exercises carried out at varying intervals.

An example cited in reference: Drill Conducted by: ABCD Public School, Greenfield Principal Acknowledgement of Completed Drill: On File at Admin Office, Acknowledgement of Completed Drill: On File at Admin Office, Fire Drill PM, #5 of 5, the School Year 2016-2017 3.21.17 @ 1:40 PM Evacuation/Shelter Time: 1 minute and 00 seconds Participants: 45 total participants Drill Conducted by: Mr Raj Bahadur, to be specific.

SAFETY & SECURITY ANCHOR

#63

Schools require more than just a watchful eye from CCTV cameras. It is critical for teachers to perform mandatory checks and become familiar with the children in their class on a first-name basis. Additionally, a HEALTH CARD that includes the kid's whole medical history must be maintained for every child.

SAFETY & SECURITY ANCHOR

#64

The school should ensure that all of the records in the journal are documented and kept up to date so that they can be easily referred to. Priority should be given to communicating with parents about any health concerns about their kids. "However, if parents and instructors do not collaborate on behalf of the student's best interests, then no school will be successful in meeting the educational needs of the students." Parents have the absolute right to know what is going on with their children while in school, and instructors should provide this information to the parents. ": - Dorothy Cohen

SAFETY & SECURITY ANCHOR

#65

Schools should promote and model responsible social interaction about technology and information; celebrate Cyber Security Week and hold activities to create awareness through cyber clubs; and advocate for and teach digital information and technology's safe, legal, and ethical use.

SAFETY & SECURITY ANCHOR

#66

Through one-on-one conversations and other forms of observational work, check for instances of cyberbullying. It is necessary to hold regular sessions on cyber ethics and make them available to students, parents, and anyone with a stake in the matter. It is necessary to implement a digital technology programme such as ERP that may work as an interactive medium "between the instructors and the guardians."

SAFETY & SECURITY ANCHOR

#67

Check on the practice of CHILD ABUSE by utilising friendly choices with the pupils by asking them to discuss their awkward situations while being with others at the school. It is up to everyone to ensure that the conditions in which our children have been raised foster self-assurance, companionship, stability, and happiness, regardless of their familial situations or backgrounds. An alert and well-informed community are necessary to protect children from potential dangers.

SAFETY & SECURITY ANCHOR

#68

Ensure employees working for the SECURITY agency have their I-Cards, lathis, umbrellas, torches, and safety belts on at all times. Every security officer who is on duty is required to have a fitness MEDICAL certificate ready for inspection.

SAFETY & SECURITY ANCHOR

#69

Any areas of the restroom or the areas around the restrooms and corridors that are prone to flooding. A necessary check on the priority is needed.

Students' health may be improved, inappropriate conduct can be discouraged, and money can be saved by having well-designed toilets in schools. The project's goal should be for the children to demonstrate these behaviours in their own homes, where they may serve as change agents in the communities in which they live.

SAFETY & SECURITY ANCHOR

#70

Floor surfaces that have been chipped or carpets in Music Rooms that are worn out and have patches or holes might make youngsters suddenly slide and become unbalanced. At the beginning of each new class, the instructor should emphasise any special safety procedures required for that particular lesson.

SAFETY & SECURITY ANCHOR

#71

Check to see that the aisles are clear of anything that could get in the way of people moving across the campus, such as trash cans, chairs, and cardboard boxes. Ensure that the classroom's natural ventilation is working correctly, that the lighting is enough, that the students are aware of the emergency evacuation drill, and that the classroom's interior flooring is in good condition. There must be rules in place in the classrooms, and ideally, those regulations should be geared toward allowing the students to establish an atmosphere of respect and accountability.

SAFETY & SECURITY ANCHOR

#72

In the classrooms, you should check to see whether the doors have stoppers. Students are responsible for monitoring their habits, and teachers are obligated to assist students in modifying these behaviours and ensuring that students comprehend that breaking the rules will result in repercussions. They should be reminded to adhere to the ground rules, and the children should not be afraid to discuss any concerns they may have.

SAFETY & SECURITY ANCHOR

OBJ

#73

Check to see that any power plugs in the classrooms, if there are any, are placed out of the children's reach. Ensure that the Earth wire is installed correctly to guard against electric shock. Telling the youngsters to keep their distance from downed power wires is a good idea. Remove any plug holes or cable holders from the wall that aren't being utilised and cover them with tape. When kids come out of the swimming pools and into the classrooms to use the computers or any other electrical item, make sure they get scorched.

SAFETY & SECURITY ANCHOR

OBJ

#74

Five S in operation, with specific markings for FAN (F) and TUBE (T) as particular mentions on switchboards inside each class. There is a need for an update check. Five Japanese words—sieri, seiton, seiso, seiketsu, and shitsuke—are referred to in the 5S way of organising a workplace, often known as the "five pillars." These have been rendered in other languages as "Sort," "Set In Order," "Shine," and "Standardize," respectively, as well as "Sustain."

SAFETY & SECURITY ANCHOR

OBJ

#75

Evaluate the MEDICAL history of the kids regularly, and as a part of the routine, instructors are required to review the child's health record in their class. It is required of him or her to keep a record of the food allergy, the physical disability, or the fact that there is a cause or case of bullying, as well as to keep the Head of the school and the Principal in the loop regarding the information that has been communicated.

SAFETY & SECURITY ANCHOR

#76

The institution IS REQUIRED to have both plan A and plan B in place for use in the event of an emergency, and its staff IS NOT PERMITTED to make judgments under pressure that they have not been trained for.

#77

Are there any messes on the Staircase, such as rubbish or spills? Ensure the youngsters always walk on the correct side of the corridors and stairs. The utilisation of the staircase will increase if it is attractive. The instructors and whoever is in charge are responsible for monitoring any slopes or falls, and sharp edges and ensuring that the maintenance is kept up to date.

SAFETY & SECURITY ANCHOR

#78

When teaching or demonstrating, do teachers or students have to stand on ladders or other platforms needing supervision and support? Under control, the aid of students may be a support system if necessary. They are gaining knowledge and experience that applies to real-world situations.

SAFETY & SECURITY ANCHOR

#79

After the assembly or when the school day is winding down, do students and teachers have permission to RUN in the area?

A necessary check and the formulation of a solution are required to facilitate a smooth and well-organized entrance and departure from the assembly ground. When the pupils are being dispersed, they need to be led. An emergency must have a public address system to guarantee a prompt and risk-free evacuation.

SAFETY & SECURITY ANCHOR

#80

The difference between safe contact and hazardous touch should be explained to children, as well as the need to avoid engagement with strangers and to communicate any concerns, regardless of how unimportant they may seem.

In addition, the parents need to be informed of any behavioural shifts that take place. There must be open lines of communication with the students, and they should be given a patient hearing for even the most insignificant of concerns.

SAFETY & SECURITY ANCHOR

#81

Students should be given a Bus Badge that includes the bus route number, and the school buses and any other school transportation should have IDENTITY markings with phone numbers for the school's help lines. They should only use the designated bus and bus stop for transportation. Both boarding and exiting the bus should be done in complete silence and according to a predetermined sequence.

SAFETY & SECURITY ANCHOR

#82

In labs and other empty spaces, computers and servers need to be monitored at all times. It is crucial to safeguard passwords and enable WIFI connections promptly for operations. Original software should be used whenever possible since it is less likely to be infected with malware or viruses. Students shouldn't be permitted to utilise any devices that plug into their computers.

SAFETY & SECURITY ANCHOR

#83

It is not appropriate for children to interact with strangers in any way. It is unacceptable to let a stranger, the driver of a vehicle, or a family friend pick up the children. It is recommended that any irregularity be reported via the Principals' hotline. Students should not be permitted to use motorised vehicles within or outside of the school grounds, including automobiles, scooters, and motorbikes.

SAFETY & SECURITY ANCHOR

OBJ

#84

When there is an emergency, do all workers know where the exits are located and how to get there? EAPs, also known as Emergency Assembly Points, must be situated some distance from the structure. Fire Exit Symbols must be installed to facilitate quick evacuation using the closest available exit route. Educational institutions must have a School Building Level Emergency Preparedness and Response Plan.

SAFETY & SECURITY ANCHOR

OBJ

#85

Are the emergency exercises scheduled regularly? Check on the training of task forces, demonstrations, and mock drills, develop an emergency resource contact inventory for human resources, transport, and tools required for dealing with emergency response, hazard hunt programmes, training for first aid search and rescue, and conducting building evacuation drills regularly. It is advised to construct a floor-by-floor thorough evacuation plan and perform a mock exercise for either an earthquake or a fire to test emergency preparations and keep the results up to date.

SAFETY & SECURITY ANCHOR

#86

Ensure all school visitors have their identities checked and the information on their IDs is thoroughly investigated. Include PARENTS as active participants and collaborators in the safety and security mechanism. Ensure that education and formal training or workshops on disaster management are provided to all relevant stakeholders to mainstream the related discipline of disaster risk management.

SAFETY & SECURITY ANCHOR

#87

Do all events and accidents get the appropriate reporting, investigation, and documentation? Check to see that the information on the school's emergency policies and procedures is provided to the parents, and make sure that the Emergency Notification Cards in the STUDENT DIARIES are kept up to date. When a crisis occurs, the plans must be carried out as an EMERGENCY plan while keeping the children safe.

SAFETY & SECURITY ANCHOR

#88

Is there quick access to medical assistance? Maintain the protocol to evacuate the building and the surrounding area, move to a temporary shelter, protect the kids and staff, inform the parents, notify the media, provide transportation, and ensure that the debriefing procedure is carried out in a timely and suitable manner. Provide the necessary TELEPHONE numbers in the event of an emergency, and have them painted and posted in visible locations around the campus.

SAFETY & SECURITY ANCHOR

#89

Enhancements. All of this must be done in the name of safety, and workers must be given the authority to question and identify any unusual visitors. In the event of an emergency, the school is required to hire a PRO, also known as a public information officer, who will be responsible for communicating information and the current state of the problem to the parents and any other parties enquiring about it.

SAFETY & SECURITY ANCHOR

#90

VISITORS Batch will be sent to everybody and everyone interested in coming to the school during business hours. In addition to this, make sure that the emergency plans are reviewed and updated regularly. Make it a live document that may be changed as necessary and promptly. The paper has to specifically include topics relating to prevention and mitigation, as well as readiness, response, and recovery.

SAFETY & SECURITY ANCHOR

#91

Ensure that an initial evaluation of the preparatory measures taken by each school building is carried out. To ensure the students' safety during evacuation, the building's layout and the adjacent areas need to be evaluated. In addition, check the equipment to ensure it will function appropriately in an emergency. Create a chain of command that can be followed in a crisis.

SAFETY & SECURITY ANCHOR

#92

Children should walk on the side of the corridors away from traffic to ensure that everyone can get to their classes without incident. Ensure that successful plans are never brought to a close. They need constant revision in light of new information garnered from experience, evolving threats, and an analysis of the state of the art's capabilities. It is necessary to perform shelter assessment requirements to prepare for various emergency responses. A stockpile of emergency supplies has to be inspected and kept up to date following its expiration date.

SAFETY & SECURITY ANCHOR

#93

Instruct youngsters and adults to RESPECT one another and get out of the way if another person is hobbling about due to an injury. Prioritizing awareness and preparation over fear should be the goal of any individual. A map indicating two different exits should be posted in every classroom throughout the school. It is crucial to ensure that the exit routes are clear and unobstructed.

SAFETY & SECURITY ANCHOR

#94

When going up and down the stairs, be sure to follow the guidelines. After everyone in the building has safely evacuated the structure

during an emergency, they should wait outside at a location that has been decided upon until they are given the "all clear" signal in the form of green light before reentering the structure.
SAFETY & SECURITY ANCHOR

#95

Include "TERRORIST THREAT" in the Curriculum of Schools.
Elementary schools up to the secondary levels need to make this topic part of their curricula, which is of the utmost importance. Students should be required to participate in it much as Israeli kids are needed to serve in the military when they are young. This is a precautionary safety measure to ensure that schools are safe and secure environments.

SAFETY & SECURITY ANCHOR

#96

Ensure that there is a SILENCE ZONE in the school so that you can keep an eye on students' behaviour and ensure that they are disciplined. The faculty and the students must follow the same religious tenets. A need that arises for every student at some point or another may easily be satisfied by instituting Quiet Zones in schools and individual classes. The need to have the ability to retreat from the din and strain of constant social engagement to refresh oneself.

SAFETY & SECURITY ANCHOR

#97

Children should be allowed to play SMART games and should follow the elementary playground safety rules. Allow the youngsters to take turns following behind you in line. Ensure that the instructors pay attention to the swings, slides, and other apparatus. They are required to provide students with active supervision while they are on the playground. Assure age-appropriate playground equipment. Only appropriate clothing for the children should be permitted, and the garden should have surfaces that absorb the impact of falls.

SAFETY & SECURITY ANCHOR

#98

Does your school have a specific location where parents can drop off and pick up their children? A designated pick-up and drop-off area for pedestrians, bus riders, and parents fetching and dropping off their children. The guided line-by-line provision needs to be a standard procedure for regular dispersal on all days, with additional provisions made for days when it may rain or when there may be an emergency. Specified Drop-offs spots are predetermined areas close to primary schools where parents are permitted to bring their children to be dropped off or picked up by the school.

SAFETY & SECURITY ANCHOR

#99

Are the safety rules posted where everyone can easily see them?

Check out the latest information about Step up for Students' Health, an initiative that promotes a healthy school environment. The schools are obligated to offer a monthly schedule to teach each kid on subjects like cleanliness, nutrition, stress, and vision via the use of instructional movies, hands-on activities, and workshops and guest lectures.

CHAPTER THREE

SAFETY- A PRIORITY

Educators, as a whole, have a duty to ensure the safety of their students and staff. They are promoting learning via an engaged culture that emphasizes safety ought to be an integral component of every classroom at all times.

A high-quality education is an absolute necessity in today's world; as a direct consequence of this, boards of teaching and learning need to work together to devise a strategy that will assist schools, teachers, and parents in educating children about the importance of responsible and secure Internet use. Encourage schools and families to locate computers in communal spaces (such as family rooms, dining rooms, workplaces, or libraries) so that children may use the Internet with other people around them. For instance, encourage schools and families to establish computers in family rooms.

In addition, instruct them never to reveal personal information (such as their name, address, telephone number, or credit card number) while using the internet. This may contribute significantly to the success of this endeavour. The day-to-day activities at school and home education will offer a healthy like for the computer, which is essential to nurture acceptable Internet usage among pre-schoolers and other young children. Home education is also required to generate a good liking for the computer.

Despite the growing use of computers in those institutions, there has not been a drop in the official teaching of handwriting in primary schools. This is another fact that might be debated. The pupils still utilise about the same amount of paper as before the widespread use of computers in educational settings. Therefore, it is essential to remember that writing with a pencil requires a set of abilities that are just as crucial as typing on a keyboard.

Children in preschool and the early primary grades may have an easier time mastering reading and other cognitive abilities when exposed to the Internet. This exposure can also stimulate an earlier integration of these skills in the child's development.

When looking for internet chances for younger children, parents and school leaders may be guided to absorb information suitable for the children's age group. Internet use may be an excellent tool for developing contact between adults and young children and reinforcing learning opportunities in daily life. Operating the new information tool effectively in this respect requires a lot of work.

Regarding computers of this kind, the work that the teaching gentry must consider is to assist teachers, parents, and children in making better use of the Internet for educational purposes. For instance, they need to recommend educational websites for parents and children to go to together. Once they get there, they need to provide the family with educational activities to participate in. Make educational assistance, such as after-school tutoring, available to kids over the internet.

Allow instructors to participate in professional development activities that will assist them in demonstrating how to make good use of the Internet as a tool for their pupils‘ learning, including incorporating Internet learning with traditional classroom learning.

If the professional development of teachers takes place outside of regular school hours, incentives should be provided to encourage instructors to attend whenever it is feasible. Suppose teachers must take time away from the classroom to participate in professional development. In that case, parents must understand the significance of supporting such initiatives.

Using the internet to interact with students and their parents is one technique to help increase everyone's interest in the subject matter. For example, create websites for the school district or individual schools, and advertise such websites in newsletters and other locations where parents are likely to congregate. Maintaining sites with material that is both relevant and up-to-date requires regular updates. Post online representative examples of students' work and teachers' comments explaining why the work satisfies academic requirements. To make websites more interactive, words may be solicited from visitors, or online public forums can be held to discuss educational concerns.

To generate pulses of excitement and interest in becoming a netizen, it is essential to encourage instructors, parents, and students to connect via email, to have their email IDs, and

even to converse offline using just that reference. And lastly, participate actively in the community.

This can be accomplished quickly and painlessly by providing convenient opportunities for parents, community leaders, teachers, and others to discuss children's Internet use. Such options include holding computer and Internet training classes for parents or hosting convenient get-togethers. Educational institutions may wish to form partnerships with other institutions that provide alternate means of accessing computers, such as public libraries, community computing centres, local colleges and universities, and other similar institutions.

References

https://www.intechopen.com/chapters/57090

https://edtechreview.in/trends-insights/insights/567-quality-education-the-ultimate-desire-by-parents

Books By The Same Author

BY NATIONAL
AWARDEE
EDUCATOR
Kindle Price: ₹ 72.00
inclusive of all taxes
Teaching
in the
VUCA
WORLD
Dr. Dheeraj Mehrotra
authordheerajmehrotra.com
Flipkart
available at
amazon

BY NATIONAL
AWARDEE
EDUCATOR
Digital List Price: ₹103.95
Kindle Price: ₹99.00
BASICS OF
ARTIFICIAL
INTELLIGENCE
&
MACHINE
LEARNING
DR. DHEERAJ MEHROTRA
authordheerajmehrotra.com
Flipkart
available at
amazon

About The Author

Dheeraj Mehrotra, MS, MPhil, PhD (Education Management) honoris causa., a white and a yellow belt in SIX SIGMA, a Certified NLP Business Diploma holder, is an Educational Innovator, Author, with expertise in Six Sigma In Education, Academic Audits, Neuro-Linguistic Programming (NLP), Total Quality Management In Education, an Experiential Educator, a CBSE Resource towards School Assessment (SQAA), CCE, JIT, Five S, and KAIZEN. He has authored over 100 books on topics which include Computer Science, AI, Digital Body Language, NLP, Quality Circles, School Management, Classroom Effectiveness and Safety and security in schools. A former Principal at De Indian Public School, New Delhi, (INDIA), NPS International School, Guwahati, and Education

Officer at GEMS, Gurgaon, with an ample teaching experience of over Two Decades, he is a certified Trainer for Quality Circles/ TQM in Education and QCI Standards for School Accreditation/ School Audits and Management.

He has also been honoured with the President of India's National Teacher Award in the year 2006 and the Best Science Teacher State Award (By the Ministry of Science and Technology, State of UP), Innovation in Education for his inception of Six Sigma In Education by Education Watch, New Delhi and Education World- Best Teacher Award, BOLT Learner Teacher Award by Air India, 'Innovation in Education Award 2016' by Higher Education Forum (HEF), Gujarat Chapter, among others. He has developed over 150 FREE EDUCATIONAL MOBILE Apps for the Google Play Store exclusively for Teachers, Students, and Parents.

This work has been recognised by the LIMCA BOOK OF RECORDS & INDIA BOOK OF RECORDS as the only Indian to draw that feast. Dr Mehrotra works as a PRINCIPAL at KUNWARS GLOBAL SCHOOL, Lucknow, in India. He has conducted over 1000 workshops globally on "Excellence In Education" integrated with Total Quality Management and Six Sigma, Technology Integration in Education (TIE), Developing towards being ROCKSTAR TEACHERS, including Cyberspace, Cyber Security, Classroom Management, School Leadership & Management, and Innovative teaching within classrooms via Mind Maps, NLP and Experiential Learning in Academics. He is an active TEDx speaker and can be viewed on the youtube TEDx channel.

As a premium UDEMY Instructor, he has developed over 450 courses and caters to over 8 Lakh students from 180 countries.

He can be visited at www.authordheerajmehrotra.com.

Printed by Libri Plureos GmbH in Hamburg,
Germany